Facts About the Eagle

By Lisa Strattin

© 2019 Lisa Strattin

Revised 2022 © Lisa Strattin

FREE BOOK

FREE FOR ALL SUBSCRIBERS

LisaStrattin.com/Subscribe-Here

BOX SET

- **FACTS ABOUT THE POISON DART FROGS**
- **FACTS ABOUT THE THREE TOED SLOTH**
  - **FACTS ABOUT THE RED PANDA**
  - **FACTS ABOUT THE SEAHORSE**
  - **FACTS ABOUT THE PLATYPUS**
  - **FACTS ABOUT THE REINDEER**
  - **FACTS ABOUT THE PANTHER**
- **FACTS ABOUT THE SIBERIAN HUSKY**

LisaStrattin.com/BookBundle

Facts for Kids Picture Books by Lisa Strattin

Little Blue Penguin, Vol 92

Chipmunk, Vol 5

Frilled Lizard, Vol 39

Blue and Gold Macaw, Vol 13

Poison Dart Frogs, Vol 50

Blue Tarantula, Vol 115

African Elephants, Vol 8

Amur Leopard, Vol 89

Sabre Tooth Tiger, Vol 167

Baboon, Vol 174

Sign Up for New Release Emails Here

LisaStrattin.com/subscribe-here

★COVER IMAGE★

https://www.flickr.com/photos/mortenholm/4345713154/

★ADDITIONAL IMAGES★

https://www.flickr.com/photos/canoehead65/4933880126/

https://www.flickr.com/photos/50885155@N05/16420347776/

https://www.flickr.com/photos/23155134@N06/11693313163/

https://www.flickr.com/photos/barrison/4414368447/

https://www.flickr.com/photos/epw/348448681/

https://www.flickr.com/photos/29638108@N06/8572350459/

https://www.flickr.com/photos/82348328@N05/14644329352/

https://www.flickr.com/photos/jitze1942/1751271668/

https://www.flickr.com/photos/15016964@N02/6159779971/

https://www.flickr.com/photos/epector/16303974141/

Contents

INTRODUCTION

The eagle is a large-sized Bird of Prey meaning that it is one of the most dominant predators in the sky. Eagles are most commonly found in the Northern Hemisphere including Europe, Asia, and North America. Eagles are also found on the African continent.

CHARACTERISTICS

Eagles exist with a dominant predatory life. They have great eyesight, pointed beaks and strong, agile feet called talons. The beak of the eagle is perfectly designed for ripping flesh away from bone, and the talons of the eagle are so strong that the eagle is able to carry prey in its feet until it reaches a safe place to eat it.

Eagles have feathers on the ends of their wings which the eagles move up and down to help them when flying.

APPEARANCE

There are more than 60 species of eagle in the world, however only two of these species are found in the USA and Canada. One of these is the most common, the Bald Eagle.

Despite the name, the bald eagle has a full head of feathers, it's just that the bright white color of the feathers makes the bald eagle very distinguishable from other eagles.

The Golden Eagle is the only other species of eagle found on the American continent.

LIFE STAGES

Female eagles build their nests in tall tree tops or high on cliffs where they can keep their eggs and eaglets safe. The mother eagle usually lays two eggs, which hatch after about one month. In many eagle species, one of the chicks is slightly stronger than the other.

LIFE SPAN

Eagles live from 15 to 30 years. Although eaglets might be preyed upon, the adult eagle is strong enough to fight off other animals.

SIZE

The size of an eagle depends upon the particular species. They range in size from 15 inches to over 3 feet in height. The wingspan of an eagle tends to be at least twice the length of the eagle's body.

HABITAT

Eagles like to be high. So, they build their nests high in treetops or cliffs. This gives them a good vantage point when looking for prey on the ground.

DIET

Eagles eat off smaller birds and bats in the sky as well as small mammals and fish on the ground. The eagle is well known for its incredible eyesight and is able to spot a mouse moving on the ground even when the eagle is still high in the sky.

ENEMIES

Eagles are dominant and ruthless predators in their environment, so they have very few natural predators. They are most likely to be hunted when they are chicks or still young and inexperienced, so they are vulnerable.

SUITABILITY AS PETS

Besides the fact that these birds are very skilled hunters and not really a good choice for a pet, it is illegal to own an eagle in many areas. It is best that you see them in preserves or watch them in the wild if you visit an area where they live. They are strong enough to carry off animals for themselves or to feed to their chicks, so the thought of having one as a pet is not the best idea.

COLOR ME

COLOR ME

COLOR ME

COLOR ME

COLOR ME

COLOR ME

COLOR ME

COLOR ME

COLOR ME

COLOR ME

Please leave me a review here:

LisaStrattin.com/Review-Vol-199

For more Kindle Downloads Visit Lisa Strattin Author Page on Amazon Author Central

amazon.com/author/lisastrattin

To see upcoming titles, visit my website at LisaStrattin.com– most books available on Kindle!

LisaStrattin.com

FREE BOOK

FOR ALL SUBSCRIBERS – SIGN UP NOW

LisaStrattin.com/Subscribe-Here

LisaStrattin.com/Facebook

LisaStrattin.com/Youtube

15317210R00026